Joining the Team

W9-CKB-722

Written by Roger Carr

Illustrated by Greg Rogers

sundance™
A Haights Cross Communications Company

🐕 a black dog book

Published by
Sundance Publishing
One Beeman Road
P.O. Box 740
Northborough, MA 01532-0740

Copyright © text Roger Carr
Copyright © illustrations Greg Rogers

First published 2001 by
Pearson Education Australia Pty. Limited
95 Coventry Street
South Melbourne 3205 Australia
Exclusive United States Distribution: Sundance Publishing

Guided Reading Level I
Guided reading levels assigned by Sundance Publishing using the text characteristics
described by Fountas & Pinnell in their book *Guided Reading*, published by Heinemann.

ISBN-13: 978-0-7608-4994-1
ISBN-10: 0-7608-4994-3

Printed in China

Contents

Characters

Megan loves sports.
She can do great tricks
with a basketball.

Nick is Megan's brother.
He loves basketball.

Joey

Angie

Peter

Bella

Duncan

Here are the members of the **Towers** team.
They are great friends.

Chapter One

The New Apartment

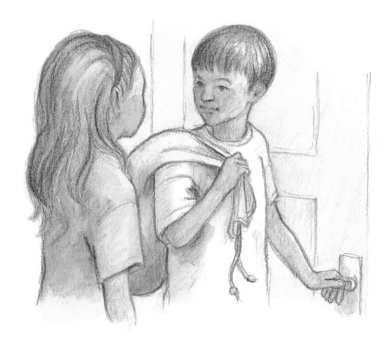

Nick lifted the laundry bag over his shoulder.
"Come on, Megan," he said.

"I wish we were at our old house," Megan said.

"So do I," said Nick. "I miss our old friends."

They had been in the apartment only one day.
They felt shy around the kids here.

Megan and Nick walked down the hall
to the laundry room.
The laundry bag bumped against Nick's back.

"Do you think we'll ever make new friends?"
said Megan.

Nick put their dirty clothes into a machine.

Megan poured in the soap.

Then they heard footsteps

and looked up.

Five kids stood in the doorway, watching them.

"I hear you made the basketball finals,"
a woman in the laundry room said to the kids.

"We're the best!" one of the boys yelled back.
Then the kids all ran off.

"Basketball finals?" asked Nick.

"Yes," said the woman.
"That's the Towers basketball team."

"Wow!" Megan said. "A basketball team.
I wish we could get to know them, Nick."

Chapter Two
Basketball Tricks

Megan's and Nick's clothes took hours to dry.

So they practiced their basketball tricks.

When they went to check on their clothes,

the Towers team was in the laundry room.

Duncan dumped some clothes out of a big bag.
He took a blue basketball uniform from the
pile and held it up.

"Look at our uniforms," he said. "I wish
we didn't have to wear them in the finals."

The uniforms were old and torn.

"Yeah, they're awful," said Bella. "I hate playing in these uniforms," she added, as she put the uniforms into a washing machine.

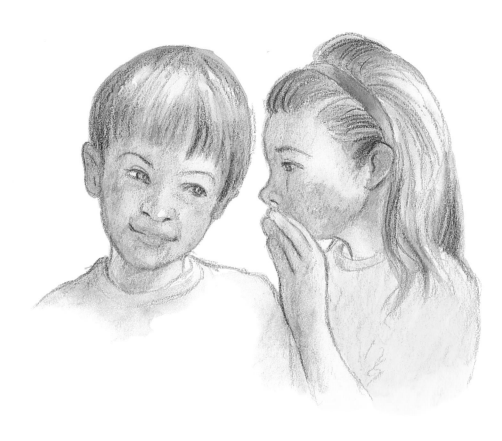

"I know how to make friends with them,"
Megan whispered to Nick. Nick listened
to Megan's plan. Then Megan bounced
her basketball in the hall.

"With uniforms like ours," said Joey,
"we should just quit the league."
Then he saw Megan standing in the doorway.
She was spinning a basketball on one finger.
It was the best trick.

"Wow, that's cool!" Duncan said.

Megan walked back into the hall
still spinning the ball.
The Towers team rushed after her to watch.

Nick waited in the laundry room
until he was sure the Towers team was gone.
Then he stopped the washing machine.
He collected the team's uniforms into a bag
and hurried away.

The Towers team kept watching Megan
spin the ball. When Megan heard Nick whistle,
she stopped spinning the ball and ran back
to their apartment. The Towers team went back
to the laundry room.

Chapter Three
No Finals

Angie opened the washing machine.

"Hey! Our uniforms are gone!" she cried.

"They're missing!" said Peter.

"Now we won't be able to play in the finals!" Duncan said.

"Look!" said Angie. "There's a trail of water!"

"Follow it!" Joey shouted.

The Towers team followed Angie down the hall.

Soon, the water trail became water spots.

Angie got down onto her hands and knees.

"It's getting harder to see them," she said.

"Quick!" said Duncan.

"Check each door before the spots dry up."

The Towers team spread out along the hall.

Duncan inspected the floor

outside Megan and Nick's door.

Then he went back to the others.

"I think it was the new kids!" Duncan said.
"There's a puddle of water on the floor."

"I bet they put our wet uniforms down
so they could open their door," said Joey.

"I've got a plan," said Bella.

The team all leaned in to listen.

Then they hid in the storage closet.

The team waited for Megan and Nick
to come by. Then they jumped out.

"Where are our uniforms?" they shouted.

"Uh, oh!" said Megan.

"Quick!" said Nick.
They turned and ran back to their apartment.

"They took the uniforms!" Bella said.

"How do you know?" Joey asked.

"The boy's back was wet," said Bella.

"We need a new plan," said Peter.

"I've got an idea," said Angie.

Chapter Four

The Uniforms

The next day, the Towers team slipped a note under Nick and Megan's door.

"We know you have our uniforms," the note said. "We want them back."

"What will we do now?" Nick asked.

Megan opened the door.
The Towers team was waiting.
"Come in and see!" Megan said.

Gran was working on the old uniforms.
"Gran's going to fix them," Megan said.

"She's sewing *TOWERS* across the front,"
said Nick.

"Hey!" Joey cried. "They look great!"

"Wow," said Duncan.
"Now we'll have the coolest uniforms."

"Yeah, thanks," said Bella.
"Maybe you two would like to play."

"Yes!" said Megan and Nick.

Chapter Five
The Big Game

Gran went with them to the finals.

Megan and Nick were on the bench.

Gran had made uniforms for them, too.

Even though Megan and Nick didn't play,
they thought it was the best game ever.